Gift Basket Guru

Starting Your Own Custom Gift-Basket Business

Table of Contents

Chapter 1. Introduction

Welcome to the wonderful world of thoughtfully curated delights! Our Special Report aptly titled "Gift Basket Guru: Starting Your Own Custom Gift-Basket Business" shines an insightful light on the fascinating and rewarding realm of customized gift-baskets. Whether you possess a flair for creativity, a love for making people happy, or simply an entrepreneurial spirit, this comprehensive guide has you covered. Positively brimming with practical tips, proven strategies, and inspiring success stories, it serves as your trusty companion on the rewarding journey of establishing a thriving, heart-touching business. Prepare to elevate your passion, cultivate unparalleled customer experiences, and ultimately unwrap the irresistible opportunity to become a renowned gift basket guru in your own right. You'll truly love what you see; don't wait, download your copy and jumpstart your dream venture today!

Chapter 2. Understanding the World of Custom Gift-Baskets

There is an intrinsic beauty woven within the fabric of the custom gift basket business, a tapestry that intertwines creativity, empathy, and business acumen. At its very heart, it seeks to capture the very essence of human emotion, transforming it into a tangible form draped in tender thoughtfulness.

2.1. The Magic behind Custom Gift Baskets

Every custom gift basket tells a story, a narrative that unfolds with each item that graces its cradle. It exudes a charm beyond the conventional borders of store-bought gifts. This exceptional allure lies in its ability to capture the individuality, taste, and spirit of the recipient, making it a truly personalized gesture of love, care, or appreciation.

Unlike off-the-shelf gifts, custom gift baskets have an uncanny knack for inducing a sense of delightful surprise. Unwrapping each item, the recipient travels on an emotional odyssey that annexes joy, astonishment, and pure elation. Interestingly, this magic is a result of the thoughtful selection and arrangement of items that struck a chord with the recipient's likings or needs.

2.2. Anatomy of a Custom Gift Basket

At the surface, a custom gift basket may seem like a simple assembly of selected items. But at its core, it is a harmonious blend of emotion, aesthetics, and purpose, designed to cater to the recipient's palate.

A gift basket typically comprises four key elements: the basket, the fillers or items, protective fill, and packaging. The basket serves as a sturdy, aesthetic base that houses the items—these could range from food items to beauty products, books, or even themed items based on one's hobbies or interests. The protective fill ensures that the items aren't damaged during transportation. Finally comes the packaging, which adds an alluring appeal to the basket, evoking anticipation and excitement.

2.3. Understanding Needs & Preferences

One of the pivotal aspects of a successful custom gift basket business is to understand the needs and preferences of your clientele. More often than not, customers are looking for unique and memorable gifts that resonate with their loved ones' interests, hobbies, or lifestyles, but may lack the time or creative flair to craft such a gift. This is where your expertise can make all the difference.

Understanding their preferences requires a discerning eye and an empathetic ear. Basic customer information like age, gender, occupation, and hobbies can provide critical insights for designing the gift basket. Also, understanding the occasion or the sentiment behind the gift aids in crafting an alluring package that echoes their emotions.

2.4. The Importance of Theming

Theme-based gift baskets have become increasingly popular in today's market. From occasions, hobbies, lifestyle choices, to dietary preferences, the opportunities are practically limitless. The themes not only enable the customisation to a granular level but also make the gift baskets more engaging and enjoyable for the recipient. Key themes could be anything from "Chocolate Lovers," "Bookworm's

Delight," "Spa Day," "Gourmand's Gourmet" to "Fitness Buff."

Creating a theme is a fun, creative process but it also requires a firm understanding of the intended recipient. Factors such as personal preferences, habits, lifestyle, preferences, dietary needs, hobbies, or merely the occasion should guide the theming process.

2.5. Leveraging Seasonality and Trends

Seasonality plays a significant role in the custom gift basket business. During holiday seasons or specific events and days such as Valentine's Day, Mother's Day, Christmas, or corporate functions, the demand for custom gift baskets sees a substantial surge.

Trends, on the other hand, offer a promising scope for innovation in your business. For example, there's a bigger emphasis on healthy living today, so naturally, more people would appreciate a basket filled with superfoods, protein bars, and vegan cosmetics.

As a proactive entrepreneur, identifying these market trends and marrying them with seasonality can reap immense rewards for your business.

2.6. Price & Profit Considerations

The profitability of your business is heavily reliant on the pricing strategy. The price should reflect not just the cost of the items but also the time, creativity, and effort that goes into crafting each basket. A proper pricing strategy requires understanding the customer's budget, market trends, and competitive pricing.

Profit generation hinges on two critical aspects: sourcing and efficiency. Acquiring items at wholesale prices improves your profit margin significantly. Cultivating relationships with local artisans or businesses might provide unique items at discounted prices. On the efficiency front, streamlining your operations – ordering, inventory management, basket assembly can contribute to cost savings, thereby increasing your profitability.

Understanding the world of custom gift baskets, then, is much more than merely knowing how to put together a beautiful basket. It spans across understanding your customer, innovative theming, leveraging seasonality, and pricing right. As you navigate this fascinating world, these insights are your bright north stars, guiding you diligently on the path of creating thoughtful, delightful gift baskets that warm hearts and smile.

Chapter 3. Exploring the Business Landscape: Market Research & Trends

Understanding the business landscape is an essential first step towards launching a successful Gift-Basket venture. This involves conducting in-depth market research and examining prevalent trends. Let's unbox this concept to pave the way for your entrepreneurial journey effectively and efficiently.

3.1. The Import of Market Research

Market research plays an indispensable role in establishing and nurturing a thriving business. This process involves gathering, analyzing, interpreting, and implementing information about your potential customers and competitors. The objective is to understand the factors that govern your target market's needs, preferences, and purchasing patterns, enabling you to steer your business decisions toward sustainable success.

1. *Identifying Your Target Market*: Your customized gift-baskets won't appeal to everyone across the board. Conducting demographic research helps identify your target audience in terms of age, gender, income, occupation, lifestyle, and geolocation. In tandem with psychographic research, this helps in comprehending your audience's tastes, preferences, and lifestyle factors to align your offerings accordingly.

2. *Understanding Your Competitors*: Competitive analysis can offer game-changing insights. Identify key players in your local area or online space and examine their strengths and weaknesses. Study their marketing strategies, pricing models, customer engagement tactics, and product range. This illuminates distinctive

opportunities to shine in your unique style and create a memorable customer experience.

3. *Forecasting Market Trends*: By examining past and present sales trends, seasonal variations, and market growth factors, you can predict future market trends. This empowers you to make strategic decisions, ensuring your offerings stay relevant and appealing.

4. *Evaluating Market Viability*: Thorough research allows you to assess the market viability for your business, gauge demand and supply dynamics, understand your cost-profit balance, and thereby validate your business idea.

3.2. Embarking on Your Market Research Journey

Now that we know the significance of market research let's outline a strategic approach to tap into this reservoir of insights effectively. Here are the action steps to follow:

1. *Define Your Research Objective*: Clear and focused research goals lay a solid foundation. This could be understanding customer needs, gauging market size, assessing competition, or predicting trends.

2. *Decide Your Research Methodology*: Depending on your objective, decide whether you need primary, secondary, or both types of research. Primary research implies firsthand data collection through surveys, interviews, focus groups, or observation. Secondary research involves examining already published data from sources like reports, studies, and online databases.

3. *Plan and Execute Your Research*: Develop a step-by-step plan for your research. If launching surveys or interviews, create your questions carefully. Be concise, clear, and ensure relevancy to your objectives. Execute your research with meticulous precision.

4. *Analyze and Interpret Data*: Once you've collected your data, the next step is to analyze it. Use statistical tools, charts, or simple spreadsheets to draw patterns and correlations. Interpret these trends relative to your research objectives.

5. *Implement Research Findings*: Finally, put your findings into action. Update your business plan, refine your product development or marketing strategy, tweak your business operations or customer engagement model based on the insights you've gleaned.

3.3. Riding the Wave of Industry Trends

Staying updated with the constant journey of trends in the gift-basket industry helps you in keeping your product offerings innovative, engaging, and relevant, thereby enhancing your business vitality.

1. *Personalization*: As consumers increasingly cherish uniqueness, gift-baskets are rightfully landing at the intersection of personalization. Crafting bespoke baskets based on individual preferences, themes, occasions, or corporate requirements is a booming trend.

2. *Health and Wellness Focus*: With wellness taking center stage, baskets incorporating healthful or organic products, fitness accessories, or wellness self-care items are gaining popularity.

3. *Sustainable and Ethical Choices*: The conscious consumerism wave translates into a preference for eco-friendly, locally sourced, fair trade, or artisanal products in gift-baskets.

4. *E-commerce and Technology Incorporation*: With digital foothold strengthening, investments in robust online platforms, AR/VR experiences, contactless delivery or IoT may define the future of this industry.

5. *Experience-Driven Gifting*: Move over material gifts; welcome

experience baskets! From gourmet cooking classes to spa vouchers, virtual art lessons to wine-tasting sessions, experiences-as-gifts is a rapidly soaring trend.

By understanding industry trends and aligning your business model accordingly, you can enhance your customers' satisfaction and loyalty, thereby driving the success and growth of your gift-basket venture. We've explored the intricate dynamics of market research and trends, now it's time to move towards creating your unique product portfolio, but that is a story for another chapter.

Chapter 4. Developing Your Unique Brand: Creativity Meets Professionalism

Creating a unique brand for your custom gift-basket business goes beyond designing a catchy logo or tagline. It's about creating a memorable impression that stays with your customers long after their purchase. Uniting your creativity with a professional approach helps to build that special brand identity.

4.1. Understanding Your Unique Value Proposition

Before you can establish your brand, you need to understand what unique value your gift-basket business can bring to your customers. What sets you apart? Is it your extensive product range, unrivaled quality, innovative basket design, or outstanding customer service? In essence, your unique value proposition (UVP) describes the distinctive benefits customers can expect when they choose your service over others. The goal is to capture this novelty, this singularity, and embed it into the DNA of your brand.

4.2. Crafting Your Brand Identity

Now that you understand your unique value proposition, the next step is to create your brand identity. This will encompass everything that represents your business and how it will be perceived in the market. From your business name, logo, color palette, typography, and packaging design to the language and tone you use in your communications, your brand identity needs to be unique, consistent, and aligned with your UVP.

Your business name should be memorable and easy to pronounce. Your logo should be simple yet catchy, reflecting the character and value of your business. Color psychology plays a critical role in driving customer emotions. Research shows that up to 90% of an initial impression about a product is based solely on color. Consequently, the colors you choose for your branded materials should evoke the feelings and emotions you want your brand to convey.

4.3. The Power of Storytelling

A powerful brand story can make your gift-basket business stand out from the crowd. Storytelling enables you to connect with your customers on an emotional level, making them feel part of your journey. It might be the story of why you started the business, a passion for the craft, or a desire to bring joy to others. Authentic, emotional, and engaging, your brand story should be infused into every aspect of your brand—from your website and social media pages to product descriptions and customer interactions.

4.4. Delivering Consistent Customer Experience

Your brand also comes to life through the experiences of your customers. Consistency is key here—consistent quality, consistent service, and consistent communication. From the moment your customer visits your website, places an order, receives your beautifully crafted gift basket, to the point they reach out for after-sales service, the experience should be seamless and consistently delightful. This consistent customer experience, combined with your unique products, forms a big part of your brand identity and reputation.

4.5. Branding and Marketing Strategy

Once you've laid the foundation of your brand, it's time to spread the word about your gift-basket business. Depending on your target customers and budget, your marketing strategy might include a mix of online marketing (SEO, PPC, social media marketing, email marketing), content marketing (blogs, articles), influencer partnerships, and traditional advertising methods.

Monitoring key metrics such as customer acquisition cost, customer lifetime value, conversion rates, customer satisfaction scores, and net promoter scores will help you gauge the effectiveness of your marketing strategies and make necessary adjustments.

4.6. Cultivating Supplier Relationships

Your suppliers play a key role in your brand's success. They are an extension of your brand. Cultivating strong, positive relationships with your suppliers will help ensure you receive quality products on time, can negotiate better deals and potentially receive unique products that set your baskets apart.

4.7. Community Engagement

Engaging with your community goes a long way in strengthening your brand. Whether it's sponsoring a local event, giving a talk about entrepreneurship at a community center, or donating a part of your profits to a good cause, community engagement not only boosts your brand visibility but also emphasizes your company's values.

4.8. A Never-Ending Journey

Finally, remember that brand development is not a one-time process—it's an ongoing journey. You should continue to listen to your customers, learn, and evolve, ensuring that your brand remains fresh, relevant, and aligned with your customers' needs and wants.

By understanding your unique value proposition, developing a consistent brand identity, crafting an engaging story, delivering exceptional customer experiences, investing in strategic marketing, cultivating supplier relationships, and engaging with your community, you can create a unique brand that stands out in the custom gift-basket business. Remember, your brand is more than just a logo—it's the heart, the personality, and the promise of your business. So, start developing your unique brand today and watch your gift-basket business thrive.

Chapter 5. Crafting Eye-Catching Designs: The Art of Basket Composition

A thriving gift basket business relies heavily on your ability to craft designs that catch the eye and capture the heart. Combining aesthetic appeal, practicality, and personalization, the art of basket composition involves careful selection and placement of items, creative use of colors, textures, shapes, and optimal utilization of the space provided. Craft your way through this journey with diligence, deftness, and a dollop of your unique style.

5.1. Understanding Your Audience

Before you start assembling your gift basket, you need to understand the needs, wants, and preferences of your intended audience. The age, gender, and personal interests of your recipient will greatly influence your selection of items, colors, and overall design. For instance, a gift basket targeting a cooking enthusiast might include gourmet ingredients, unique utensils, or a hardcover cookbook. Understanding your audience and their preferences will allow you to create a gift basket that's truly relatable, unique, and treasured.

5.2. Selecting the Right Basket

The first critical consideration when composing your gift basket is the actual container. While traditional willow baskets have a universal appeal, you could consider using containers that enhance the overall theme of your gift or can be repurposed. Wooden crates, ceramic bowls, or metallic tins can make your gift basket stand out while adding an extra layer of usability. Ensure that the size of your container is just right - too much space would make it appear empty, while not enough can make it cramped.

5.3. On-theme Item Selection

The content is key to a standout gift basket. Items should not only align with the preferences of your recipient but should also form a cohesive unit. This can be achieved by selecting a clear theme for your basket. Whether it's "Chocolate Indulgence", "Tropical Delight", or "Spa Retreat", having a theme allows your gift basket to tell a story that resonates deeply with its intended recipients.

5.4. Basket Composition and Arrangement

The arrangement of items within your basket can either make it aesthetically pleasing or give it a cluttered appearance. Begin by arranging larger items first for stability and balance. Then, gradually integrate smaller items, ensuring each piece is visible. You could make use of props like tissue paper, shred, or foam as needed for padding, stability, and visual appeal. Further, an aspect of your arrangement can also be organic, where you allow the arrangement to grow dynamically based on each item's shape, size, and color.

5.5. Adding a Splash of Color

Colors play an essential role in creating visual appeal. Firstly, consider whether you want your basket to be vibrant and colorful, or more subtle and elegant. Use color combinations that are pleasant to the eye, focusing on harmonious arrangements rather than bursts of dissimilar hues. Focus on coordinating colors of basket contents, container, and packaging tying them together tastefully.

5.6. Adding Texture

Texture provides an extra layer of intrigue to a gift basket, inviting the recipient to not only look but also touch and engage with the gift. Play with a variety of texture - chunky knits, silky ribbons, rustic wood, smooth ceramics - to create a multi-faceted sensory experience.

5.7. Topping Off with Beautiful Packaging

Packaging is the final touch that can make a big difference to your gift basket. Cellophane wraps are a popular choice, providing a protective cover while still allowing the items to be seen. Decorative elements like ribbons, tags, or labels add a personal touch. Also, handwritten notes of appreciation or greeting make your gift seem more personalized.

5.8. Consistent Branding

Remember that each basket you design is a reflection of your brand. Consistency in quality, design scheme, or even certain elements that become your signature style can help your business stand out from the competition.

Building alluring gift baskets is a multidimensional task that involves weaving together various facets into a coherent, engaging product that is not merely an assembly of items, but a thoughtfully crafted delight in its own right. As you continue on this path, refining your style and understanding your customer needs better with each creation, the art of basket composition becomes a rewarding practice.

Remember, the aim is to create baskets that enchant the recipients with their charm and thoughtfulness; baskets that echo your core beliefs; baskets that the world hasn't seen before. That is the art of basket composition, and that is what will set you apart as a true gift basket guru. Now, equip yourself with these insights, and start creating marvels, one gift basket at a time.

Chapter 6. Choosing the Right Products: Sourcing & Selection

One of the greatest thrills of crafting a custom gift basket business is homing in on the perfect items. The selection process requires an attentive eye, an ear to your market's needs, and a keen understanding of the value your products offer. This endeavor extends beyond stocking pleasing goods to providing a delightful, personalized experience for your target customer. Let's dive into the world of product sourcing and selection with a keen focus on choosing the rights items for your gift-basket business.

6.1. Understanding the Market Needs

To provide gift baskets that truly resonate with your customers, understanding your market is a vital initial step. This process involves tapping into your domain knowledge and implementing strategic market research.

Before deciding on which products to include, conduct comprehensive research about your target audience. Determine their needs, preferences, and buying behavior. This will give you insights into what your customers would likely enjoy. Keep on top of cultural, social, and industry trends. These can be a treasure trove of useful ideas and inspiration for your chosen items.

6.2. Curating for Occasions and Themes

Custom gift baskets appeal to customers because they offer personalized, one-stop shopping for various occasions. Selecting products won't simply be about what's delightful or popular. It requires strategic planning based on occasions and themes.

Holidays, celebrations, and personal life events form a significant part of your calendar. Each brings its unique sentiment that the chosen products should echo. For a Christmas basket, traditional items like holiday cookies, ornaments, and scented candles could be chosen. A wellness-themed basket, on the other hand, might contain items like green tea, an essential oil diffuser, and a yoga book.

6.3. Quality vs. Cost

Quality and cost are key considerations when sourcing and selecting items. High-quality products can enhance your brand reputation, while cost influences the profitability of your business.

Always sample prospective products, evaluate packaging, and research the manufacturers to ensure quality. For cost, consider the retail price, shipping fees, minimum order requirements, and discounts for bulk purchasing.

It is important to strike a balance — what fits the budget may not always uphold the quality standards you strive to meet. The rule of thumb should be that you're comfortable gifting the items in question to loved ones. This mindset will help you assess whether the cost justifies the quality.

6.4. Sourcing Products

Choosing the right supplier is as critical as selecting the right products. The right supplier not only ensures steady inventory but also influences the quality and cost of your products.

To start, list down potential suppliers you can find online, through trade shows, or industry and networking events. Reach out directly to the manufacturers or use a reliable wholesaler directory.

When evaluating suppliers, assess their reliability, quality of products, shipping costs and duration, minimum order requirements, return policies, and willingness to provide samples.

6.5. Building Relationships with Suppliers

Cultivating a good relationship with your suppliers ensures smoother operations for your business. It can lead to preferential prices, better cooperation in accommodating sporadic large orders, faster responses, and even exclusive deals.

Connect with your suppliers regularly, treat them as important stakeholders in your business, appreciate their good service, and promptly address any issues.

6.6. Aligning Products with Your Brand

Your product selection should align with your brand identity. If your brand promotes organic and natural living, including items that are mass-produced or artificially flavored can mislead your customers and dilute your brand.

Consistency in your brand message promotes trust and loyalty among your customers, which will contribute to the success and growth of your business.

6.7. Legal and Regulatory Considerations

Any products you choose must comply with the relevant laws and regulations. This can include food safety standards, labeling requirements, and bans on certain substances.

Ensure you're aware of the necessary regulations in the areas you operate in, particularly for food and skincare items, for a seamless business operation.

6.8. Monitoring and Adjusting Your Product Selection

Product selection isn't a one-and-done task. It requires ongoing monitoring and adjusting based on customer feedback, market trends, product performance, and changes in your suppliers' circumstances.

Maintain an open mind and be willing to adjust your product range to meet new customer demands or respond to any unexpected changes.

Finalizing your product selection is an evolving process, colorful and multilayered, just like the array of potential items for your baskets. Choosing the right items requires researching, strategizing, and being astute with sourcing. This chapter should assist you in crafting an irresistible, varied, and high-quality selection that's sure to dazzle customers and establish your reputation in the thrilling realm of the custom gift basket business.

Chapter 7. Establishing Target Audience: Know Your Customers

Understanding the specifics of your target audience is the cornerstone of establishing a fruitful gift basket business. Done correctly, this process allows you to build targeted marketing campaigns and create basket designs tailoring to customers' preferences, thereby enhancing customer satisfaction and bolstering your overall success.

7.1. The Importance of Knowing Your Customers

Essentially, the goal of any business is to satisfy customers. For a gift-basket business, understanding the needs and wants of your customer base is imperative. Consider this: You wouldn't offer a fruit basket to someone who's allergic to fruits, would you? Your offerings should be a reflection of what your customers desire or require.

Knowing your customers aids in forming a more personal connection and fostering loyalty. It allows you to be proactive in fulfilling their needs, setting the right prices, and putting forth an appropriate marketing strategy. Moreover, when you get the gift basket right, the chances of a customer recommending your business to their peers increase, boosting your client base and business prospects.

7.2. Identifying Your Customers

The journey of understanding your target audience begins with one critical task: identification. You should be able to answer significant questions including but not limited to: Who are they? What do they do? What are their interests?

Common parameters for identification include: 1. Demographic Information: This pertains to age, gender, occupation, income level, and marital status among other factors. 2. Geographic Location: Are your customers locals or based internationally? Where exactly are they? 3. Lifestyle and Preferences: Are your customers health-conscious, luxury-seeking, or eco-friendly? Will they prefer themed baskets or prefer the classics?

Creating customer profiles or 'personas' using this information can aid in tailoring your offerings and marketing techniques effectively.

7.3. Gathering Information

Once you have an idea of who your potential customers might be, the next step is to gather more precise and detailed data. This could be accomplished in several ways:

1. Surveys: These are concise, structured questionnaires targeting specific aspects of customer behavior. They could be administered face-to-face during expos and conventions, or digitally through email and social media.

2. Observations: See first-hand how customers interact with similar products. Pay attention to popular basket themes, pricing, occasions, and buying habits.

3. Customer Feedback: Encourages communication with your customers to understand their needs better. This could be accomplished through direct communication or feedback forms.

4. Competitor Analysis: Glean insights into what your competitors are doing right and where they could improve. Learning from their successes and failures can help you as you shape your business.

7.4. Analyzing Information

After collecting substantial information about your customers, the next course of action is to analyze this data to gather meaningful insights. Identifying patterns and trends within the data can reveal significant aspects about customer preferences.

Successful analysis should aid in clarifying the following: 1. Which gift basket themes are popular? 2. What price range are customers comfortable with? 3. What occasions do they mostly buy gift baskets for? 4. Which marketing channels resonate best with them?

The analytics gleaned here should influence the decision-making process of your business, from product development to marketing strategies.

7.5. Responding to Customer Behaviour

Knowing your customers isn't a one-time event. People change and grow, and so do their tastes and preferences. Keeping track of evolving trends can fortify the longevity and relevance of your business.

By nurturing a responsive and adaptable business model, you cater to emerging customer needs, thereby maintaining a loyal customer base whilst attracting new clientele.

7.6. Leveraging Information for Profit

The end goal of knowing your customers is, ultimately, to maximize profit. Leveraging the knowledge of your customers will enable you to create targeted marketing campaigns, design specific gift baskets, and set the right price points to attract and retain your customers. Remember—the more you customise, the more you profit.

The focus should be on establishing a unique selling proposition (USP) that differentiates you from your competitors. By aligning this USP with the wants and needs of your target market, you can build a strong, identifiable brand that stands out in the gift basket industry.

Knowing your customers is inevitably a rewarding journey that significantly influences the success of your business. As you embark on this voyage of exploration, remember to be flexible and adaptable, always willing to meet your customers wherever they are. In doing so, you create a thriving, sustainable business that benefits everyone involved, and you position yourself as a trusted gift basket guru in your customers' hearts.

Chapter 8. Pricing for Profit: Financial Management Principles

Entering the world of gift baskets is not just about the joy of creating aesthetically pleasing and thoughtful presents. It's also about effectively managing the business aspect to ensure profitability and sustainability. Indeed, one of the essential aspects of your venture's success will be understanding pricing and maintaining a keen grip on financial management principles.

8.1. Understanding the Cost of Goods Sold

First and foremost, understanding the cost of goods sold (COGS) is fundamental. This represents the direct costs of producing your gift baskets. The COGS includes the costs for materials used to assemble the basket, such as the basket itself, the items that will fill the basket, any wrapping or decoration material, plus the labor cost associated with creating the basket.

Calculate the COGS for each gift basket like so:

```
Cost of items (basket, filler items, decoration) + Labor
costs
```

Effectively tracking COGS will provide invaluable insights into the products' profitability and the overall financial health of your business.

8.2. Spending Wisely: The Art of Strategic Purchasing

Bulk purchasing can potentially reduce your costs tremendously, contributing to increased profit margins. However, balance is key. Buying too much can lead to a surplus of perishable goods, or tie up capital unnecessarily. Before making a purchase, ask:

- Will the items remain fresh (in case of perishable goods)?

- Can I quickly sell this volume of gift baskets?

- Do I have enough storage room for these goods?

Develop relationships with suppliers that can provide regular, reliable service. This may offer opportunities for volume discounts and better pricing terms.

8.3. Deciding a Market Price

Research is your friend when it comes to determining your market price. Understand what competitors are charging for similar baskets and learn what customers are willing to pay. A key principle to remember is 'value-based pricing'. This means pricing your baskets based on what customers think they're worth, rather than simply the cost. Bear in mind that people pay for the value they perceive. Your baskets offer not only useful goods, but also convenience, aesthetics and the feeling of giving a thoughtful gift. These aspects all add value and should be considered when setting the price.

8.4. Calculating the Markup

Once the COGS is determined, and the desired profit margin identified, it's time to calculate a markup. This will cover your overheads (indirect costs, such as rent and utilities) and determine your selling price.

Firstly, calculate your overhead percentage based on your current costs:

```
(Overhead Costs / Total Sales) * 100
```

Next, determine your desired profit margin. If aiming for a 20% profit, deduct this from 100% (left for the COGS and overhead). Here's how to get the markup percentage:

```
100% ▯ Desired Profit Margin (20%) ▯ Overhead Percentage
```

Then use this formula:

```
Selling Price = (COGS / (100% - Markup Percentage)) *
100
```

Bear in mind that this gives a 'minimum price'. Adjust this according to perceived customer value and competitor pricing.

8.5. Adjustments and Discounts

There might be times when giving discounts will attract customers, increase sales volumes or clear out stock. However, there is a real cost to discounts; be certain you understand your profit margins thoroughly before offering any markdowns.

8.6. Financial Tracking and Review

Effective financial management goes beyond setting the right price. It also involves regularly tracking sales, expenses, and cash flow.

Regularly review your financial data, look for trends, and adjust pricing or costs if needed.

In conclusion, pricing is both an art and a science. Knowing your costs is essential, but so is understanding the value customers perceive in your baskets. To run a successful gift basket business, you must balance financial principles with keen market insight and customer understanding.

Chapter 9. Marketing Your Business: Strategies for Success

The most important aspect of any business is how it is perceived by its consumers. If we consider our business-like creating a gift, marketing is the wrapping that gives it allure. With the right marketing strategies, a small startup can compete with bigger corporations, and a local venture can reach worldwide.

9.1. Crafting a Brand Identity

Crafting your brand identity is like creating the personality of your enterprise. This is not only about developing a logo or tagline but defining what your business stands for, its values and unique selling points - what sets you apart from the competition.

Your crafted brand identity should reflect in all your business activities - from the design and quality of your gift baskets to customer service and your online presence. It must be consistent across all platforms, both digital and physical, to foster reliability and trust with your customers.

9.2. Building a Robust Online Presence

We live in a digital age where most people resort to online platforms for convenience. A robust online presence is vital to increase your visibility and reach.

Website: A professional website is an online storefront showcasing everything your business has to offer. It needs to be user-friendly, visually appealing, and informative. Include images of your products, detailed descriptions, prices, and how to place orders. Make sure it is optimized for mobile viewing, as a significant proportion of customers shop from their smartphones.

Social Media: Harness the power of social media to create brand awareness and connect with your target audience. Regularly post engaging content on platforms your target audience frequents - be it Instagram, Facebook, Pinterest, Twitter, or LinkedIn. Respond promptly to comments and messages to cultivate engagement.

9.3. Traditional Marketing Methods

While digital marketing is a powerful tool, traditional marketing methods like flyers, business cards, billboards, and word-of-mouth advertising can still strike a chord with local consumers. Building alliances with local businesses and attending community events can create a buzz around your business and gather a loyal customer base.

9.4. Email Marketing

Building an email list allows you to market directly to interested customers. You can send personalized deals, new product launches, event invitations, and newsletters. Make sure every email provides value to keep your subscribers interested; otherwise, they might unsubscribe. Emphasize the "opt-in" strategy to ensure your subscribers genuinely want to receive your emails.

9.5. Search Engine Optimization (SEO)

Create a blog on your website to share helpful content about your products and the gifting industry. This not only provides value to your customers but also helps in optimizing your website for search engines. Use relevant keywords and phrases in your content that potential customers might search for. Good SEO practices will improve your website's ranking in search engine result pages, increasing visibility and attracting organic traffic to your site.

9.6. Collaborations and Partnerships

Collaborations can boost brand awareness further. Consider partnering with companies that compliment your offerings. For example, establish an affiliate relationship with a local florist or gourmet food store. Similarly, organizing contests or giveaways with influencers who cater to a similar demographic as you can offer promotional benefits.

9.7. Customer Feedback and Referrals

Customer feedback is vital not just for product and service improvement but also for marketing. A happy customer's review can sway prospective buyers and build your company's credibility. You can include an incentive, like a small discount on their next order, to encourage customers to leave reviews.

9.8. Paid Advertising

Paid advertising comes in many forms including pay-per-click (PPC), social media ads, sponsored blog posts, and more. Define your target audience, budget, and objectives to devise a well-structured paid advertising campaign. This can help in spreading brand awareness, driving website traffic, and boosting sales.

9.9. Measuring Success

Lastly, it is crucial to measure the results of your marketing efforts. Metrics like customer acquisition cost, conversion rate, customer lifetime value, and return on investment can provide insights on which strategies are working and which need tweaking.

Invest in analytics tools to gather data and adjust your marketing strategies accordingly. Also, keep an eye on market trends and consumer behavior to update your strategies timely.

In conclusion, successful marketing for your gift-basket business relies on combining digital and traditional strategies, maintaining consistency, engaging with your audience, and continuously measuring your results. Remember, the most compelling part of your brand is the love and thoughtfulness put into each basket. It is your unique selling point, and your marketing strategies should highlight it.

Chapter 10. Customer Service Excellence: Nurturing Relationships

While the artistry of creating meticulously curated gift baskets is critical, another dimension that cannot be overlooked is the quality of your customer service. To truly nurture relationships and achieve customer service excellence, you must go beyond merely a transactional exchange and endeavor to engage your provision of service on a personal level, creating lasting, impactful experiences.

10.1. The Personalisation Paradigm

Personalisation in customer service is not a new idea, but in the world of custom gift baskets, it's an obvious differentiator. The ability to tailor gifts for each individual customer allows for a level of personal touch that elevates the gift-giving experience. This personal attention must extend to customer service as well.

Whenever communicating with your clients, be it over phone, email, or in-person, show genuine interest in their needs and desires, listen carefully, and provide thoughtful responses. Remember their preferences, and use that information in future interactions. A customer who feels known and understood is much more likely to become a loyal patron.

10.2. Emotional Intelligence: Pillar of Service Excellence

Emotional intelligence in customer service is the ability to understand, use, and manage your own emotions in positive ways to relieve stress, communicate effectively, empathize with others, overcome challenges and defuse conflict.

When faced with an upset or irate customer, take a moment to put yourself in their shoes. This can provide the perspective needed to handle the situation with empathy and grace. By showing understanding and patience, you turn a potentially negative interaction into a chance to reinforce the resilience and professionalism of your business.

Remember, emotions are contagious. Convey positivity, calmness, and approachability at all times. A smile, even over the phone, can set the tone for an entire interaction.

10.3. Develop a Customer-Focused Culture

Your team is vitally important in achieving customer service excellence. Hire people who align with your commitment to superior service, and instill in them the value of making every customer interaction exceptional. Regular training sessions can provide essential skills for employees to handle various customer service scenarios efficiently and professionally.

Make sure your staff understand the importance of going the extra mile. Whether it's following up on orders, rectifying mistakes swiftly, or merely remembering client preferences - these seemingly small acts can make a significant impact on your relationship with your customers.

10.4. Feedback: The Catalyst for Improvement

No one knows better about the areas you need to improve than your customers. Use surveys, social media, and direct conversations to gather feedback about their experiences with your service, product quality, delivery, and more.

Use this feedback constructively. Acknowledge the criticism, thank your customers for their input, and work on fixing any issues. Even negative reviews can offer valuable insights into areas you might need to improve.

10.5. Rewards and Recognition: Foster Loyalty

Loyal customers are invaluable assets. Showing appreciation towards your returning clients can be an effective way to fortify these relationships. Develop a rewarding loyalty program, offer special discounts, seasonal offers, or simply a thank you note with their orders. Small gestures of recognition can leave a lasting impression, often leading to positive word-of-mouth and referrals which are critical for your business growth.

10.6. The Art of Dealing with Complaints

At some point, you're bound to face customer complaints. How well you manage them can distinguish you as a business that truly values its customers.

When faced with a complaint, listen first. Understand the issue from the customer's perspective. Apologize genuinely, not just for the issue, but for the inconvenience it caused. Once the problem is clearly defined, offer a solution, and assure the customer that steps will be taken to prevent such issues in the future.

10.7. Building Trust through Transparency

To establish strong customer relationships, trust is key. One way to build trust is by being transparent about your business processes. Let your customers behind the scenes - show them how you source materials, select items for their baskets, and work meticulously to meet their specifications. Being transparent about delays, issues, or even mistakes can be better appreciated than hiding them.

10.8. Ensure Convenient Customer Experience

Efficient service is a cornerstone of customer satisfaction. Make every process - from ordering, customization, payment, to delivery - as simple and seamless as possible. A customer who experiences convenience at every step will likely have a positive opinion about your service.

In the end, achieving customer service excellence comes down to genuinely caring about your customers. Embody this in your communications, in your actions, and in your products. With consistency and dedication, you can emerge as a thought-leader in the gift basket business, set apart by extraordinary service and cherished relationships.

Chapter 11. Maintaining Success: Growing & Scaling Your Business

Success in business means not only establishing a robust foundation but also continuously growing and scaling to meet an ever-evolving demand. Your creative gift-basket business is not an exception. After you've successfully launched and provided numerous clients with customized happiness, maintaining the achieved success and scaling it further is a requisite for long-term profitability and sustainability in this industry.

11.1. Sustainable Growth Strategy

Growth is vital for any business, but it needs to be sustainable and not sporadic. It's about developing a step-by-step plan that projects growth in a manageable and responsible way. Unregulated growth could result in chaos, making it hard to manage orders, causing a decline in quality, or leading to customer dissatisfaction.

Firstly, understand your business's current stage and where you want to take it. Visualize your objectives clearly. You may want to diversify your offering, replicate successful initiatives in new markets, or perhaps aim for a bigger share of the current market. Setting clear trajectories will make it easier to plan your objectives and track your progress.

11.2. Learning From Customer Feedback

As the saying goes, the customer is always right. Ensure that you're constantly evaluating customer feedback. Their opinions offer an unbiased appraisal of what's working and what needs improvement. Constructive criticism is an opportunity to enhance your service, design, quality, and overall process. Using customer surveys or maintaining an open channel for feedback encourages customers to voice their experiences, and their insights can provide you invaluable ways to expand and improve.

11.3. Strengthening Brand Presence

Building a strong brand is crucial. Apart from exquisitely designed gift baskets, think about what your brand represents — its personality, its unique value proposition. This is an ongoing process, evolving as your business matures.

Increasing brand visibility is integral to growth. This can be done through a more extensive online presence via social media marketing, SEO, and an informative, user-friendly website. Invest in professional photos of your baskets, and share customer testimonials and success stories for a greater impact.

Holding events like interior design workshops or gift-making classes can further cement your brand in the local community. Partnering with local businesses for these events can provide additional networking opportunities and access to a broader clientele.

11.4. Expanding Your Product Range

One way to maintain your business's success while ensuring its continued growth is by expanding your product range. This could involve including baskets for specific occasions, like baby showers or graduations, or offering a variety of themed baskets, such as wine and cheese, book lovers, or spa baskets. You could also venture into corporate gifting, a segment that promises good returns.

Ensure you perform market research to understand what potential customers are seeking. Test any new offerings with a limited rollout before committing fully.

11.5. Investing in Innovative Technology

In the modern world, technology can be the catalyst that launches your business's growth to new heights. Targeted advertising on social media platforms can attract new customers while email marketing can keep your business on the top of current customers' minds.

Incorporating software to manage orders, deliveries, inventory, and accounting will streamline your business operations, freeing up time for more strategic work.

11.6. Building a Team

As your business grows, it will become challenging to handle all tasks by yourself. Hiring a reliable and competent team to manage tasks such as sourcing materials, production, marketing, and customer service will help you scale more effectively.

11.7. Conclusion

Always remember, maintaining success is an enduring process, not an endpoint. It requires continuous effort, adaptation, and iteration based on market dynamics. Keep refining and modifying your business strategy, consider diversifying your product range, embrace technology to streamline operations, and don't be shy in seeking professional help where needed. Stay agile, passionate, and customer-centric, and you'll see your gift-basket business reach heights you never imagined.